Comments on Gerry Maguire Thompson's work:

*"I read the book to our cats and dogs. My wife
and our rabbit listened too. It has helped us all."*
BERNIE SIEGAL, AUTHOR OF "LOVE, MEDICINE AND MIRACLES"

"This'll make you laugh even if you hate pets"
HILARY BOYD, THE EXPRESS

"Great swing and relish"
SEAMUS HEANEY, NOBEL PRIZEWINNER AND POET

"Loved it – very funny"
SUE TOWNSEND, AUTHOR OF THE ADRIAN MOLE BOOKS

"Witty and informative"
TIME OUT MAGAZINE

"I wish that boy would get a proper job"
AUTHOR'S MUM

No humans were harmed in the making of this book

CONVERSATIONS
WITH DOG

*Instructions
for Life Channelled
from Above*

A PARODY BY GERRY MAGUIRE THOMPSON

 A GODSFIELD BOOK

To Seffy with appreciation

First published in Great Britain in 2000
by Godsfield Press Ltd
A division of David and Charles Ltd
Winchester House,
259-269 Old Marylebone Road,
London, NW1 5XJ, UK

10 9 8 7 6 5 4 3 2 1

© 2000 Godsfield Press
Text © Gerry Maguire Thompson

Designed for Godsfield Press by
The Bridgewater Book Company

Illustrations by Madeleine Hardie

Printed in Italy - Nuova GEP, Cremona

ISBN 1-84181-102-5

CONTENTS

INTRODUCTION

I'd like to tell you the incredible story of how this book came about. A couple of years ago, my life was in a real mess. My marriage had fallen apart and my wife had left me. I felt betrayed and abandoned. I lost my job, and just sat around at home all day feeling miserable. My friends stopped speaking to me. I couldn't sleep at night, and had no appetite. I felt like I had lost everything – all that was left was my loyal and trusty dog Virgil. I just couldn't understand it. Why was this happening to me? What was the point of it all? Was it worth going on with life?

Then, suddenly, I had a brilliant idea: I'd write to God and get answers to all these questions, and to other questions too.

Questions like "Where did I go wrong?", "How can I be happy?", "Why is the world such a bad place?" and "What can I do to make my ex-wife's life hell?". I sent about a hundred such letters, but I didn't get a single reply. So then I asked my dog instead. And an amazing thing happened – I got answers straight away! The information contained in them was simply incredible. It was as if my dog was channelling messages to me from some higher source; I now know that they came from an extraordinary disembodied and all-knowing canine divinity, known only as "Dog". This amazing book, then, is a record of all my questions about life – and a lot more that I didn't realise that I needed to ask – and of Dog's profound and transformative answers. I make no bones about it: this book will change your life, too.

PAWS FOR THOUGHT

As soon as I'd made this discovery, everything began to change. Whenever something was bothering me, I'd sit down and ask Dog about it. Pretty soon I'd hear that strange, otherworldly voice coming out of the depths of the cosmos. It was compassionate, yet authoritative and sometimes stern; gruff, and a little husky. Dog's messages would vary widely in their tone, ranging from the awe-inspiring to the seemingly mundane. Sometimes Dog would encourage me with warm words of support and succour; and at other times he would reproach me for the mess I was making of things. Nor was Dog always serious – often he would make me laugh out loud with his mixture of wit and wisdom.

But always his words were deep and meaningful, and always they had a profound effect on my life.

🐾 As a result, the circumstances of my life have been completely transformed. I'm now happy, healthy and totally fulfilled. My needs are simpler, and I am free from worries. I go out all the time. I adore any kind of exercise. I have an incredible appetite. When there isn't much going on, I just lie down and go to sleep until the next interesting thing happens. My sense of smell is amazing. And I'm no longer depressed about being single – in fact, I'm meeting lots of new people and having plenty of sex in public places. Best of all, I just heard that my ex-wife is having a terrible time, and wants me back – but no way!

🐾 And so it is my dearest wish that you, too, will be able to benefit from the extraordinary wisdom in this book, and that it will help you on your spiritual path. I guarantee that this incredibly inspirational material will turn you into a completely different person.

BARKING UP THE WRONG TREE

Immediately I discovered that I could talk to Dog, the very first questions that I asked him were: "Who are you? Why are you here? And how come you didn't talk to me before?" The answers came at once, with devastating power and clarity:

"I have been speaking to you through my emissaries for all of your life, but you have not been listening. I have been seeking to teach you my lessons and my truths, yet you have not heeded what I have tried to show you. Instead, you have treated me as a likeable but lowly form of life, someone who is there just to make your own life a little less miserable.

"It is the same with all of you upright-walking beings. You have completely misunderstood my message, delivered to you from time immemorial

through your domesticated canine allies. You think that I have been provided just to come when you whistle, to carry out demeaning tasks, to bring the newspaper from the shop, or to bite strangers when they break into your dwelling in the middle of the night. Or perhaps you think I am some sort of status symbol, or maybe a means for getting into conversations with attractive walkers who wander around in the park with their own canine accessories.

"But I have far more than this to offer you. I am actually here to teach you fundamental lessons about spirituality, and about the ultimate purpose of your existence. Through me, you can come to understand the true essence of your being, and so gain real and lasting fulfilment.

"As human beings, you are spiritually very lazy. You treat the whole of life as if it were an enormous living room where you can spend the whole time sitting around idly, watching television. But my wisdom can lead you away from these negative patterns – no longer will you vegetate in this way.

"My inherent nature will inspire you by its example, for my spirit is that of unconditional love and wholehearted dedication. I am here to set you free, to let you off the self-imposed leash that holds you back in life. I am here to show you, the whole human race, who you really are. All this I will give you, and more.

🐾 "I can tell you where the real spiritual 'meat' in life is to be found; I will indicate where the true bones of enlighten-ment are buried. I shall show you how to trust your instinct, to follow your nose and sniff out the Ultimate Truth of the Universe itself.

🐾 "You've heard that you now live in the digital age. Well, the next age of humanity will be known as the 'dogital age'. During this era, your species will learn all the lessons that I have been teaching you, and manifest all the attributes of canine enlightenment.

🐾 "And yet I know that you will always want to stay with your old ways, because you do not understand your true relationship with me. It will be hard for you to realise the painful truth of the matter – that it is not you who are leading me through life, but I who am leading you. It is not you who is training me to carry out your petty little chores; it is I who am training you for the highest purpose that life can offer. I am here to

improve you and to socialise you; to help you transcend your unacceptable and destructive habits, and to get you to behave responsibly.

🐾 "But I cannot hand all this information to you on a plate, for that would be treating you like a puppy; and what I want is for you to truly grow up. So you must try to understand what I will be saying to you through the medium of metaphor and allegory. You must translate my words into your own terms in order to discern their profound truth. I know that you can do this – you and all the many millions of readers who will one day come to hear this message. At times you will think that I am barking mad, but in the end you will understand. And you will be truly happy."

DIGGING FOR ENLIGHTENMENT

It all sounded incredible, wonderful and amazing. All I had to do was to ask the right questions, and I would be able to solve any problem. And not only my own problems, but also those of the whole of humanity. I could find out all I ever wanted to know – or anything anyone ever wanted to know about anything. I was sure that people would give a lot for this information. I could make money out of it. I could become rich and famous, and incredibly influential. And very spiritual. But where to start? What was to be my first request? There was so much I wanted to know.

🐾 So I started with this question:

ME: "How can I become the most incredibly powerful person in the world, amazingly happy and fulfilled, modest, and loved by everyone? And have a nice girlfriend as well?"

🐾 I waited for an answer. There was only silence. I panicked. Was my query not a good one to start with? Had I already come up with a question to which Dog did not know the answer? Had I somehow blown it, already?

🐾 The silence continued. Then at last I heard the beginnings of a sound – a deep, resounding rumble, a sort of cosmic canine sigh. Then words began to be formed:

DOG: "Oh dear me. Oh dearie dearie me. Is this really what you want to know, of all the things in the universe that you could ask me? Well, I'm afraid you've got the wrong end of the spiritual stick. You humans have been doing this since the beginning of time. No wonder your whole species is forever going round in circles, chasing your own tails and making a dog's dinner out of world affairs. With you people, it's always *me, me, me*, isn't it? Can't you ask about something else, at least to start with?"

ME: "Okay, tell me a bit about yourself."

DOG: "Good. I thought you'd never ask. Well, let's put it this way. I'm the ultimate incarnation of all higher canine energies in the universe. In all universes, in fact. I am the leader of the cosmic pack, as it were.

"You humans, in your humano-centric arrogance, think of all higher powers as being just like yourselves, but this is not so. Some higher entities are indeed human-like. But others are feline, or aquatic. There is also a great deity known as Mouse. There's even an entity called Jellyfish – a very good friend of mine, actually. All the forms on Earth have their own associated higher beings. And we all have something to teach you. Yet your Western creation mythology teaches nothing of our Being. Only the Native Americans acknowledge me, calling me 'Coyote', or the 'Great Trickster'. I quite like that.

🐾 "But my inherent being is threefold: Dog the Father, Dog the Son and Dog the Hairy Spirit. This last part of me is what you know best; it has manifested itself among you on Earth, in what you think of as your so-called 'pet dogs'. These are my emissaries. You must listen to them, and learn what they have to teach you. Follow their example. Draw inspiration from them. Feel inside you that which resonates with their teachings; connect with your own inner dog. That is what these conversations with me will enable you to do. Then you will be truly fulfilled."

ME: "Wow!"

DOG: "But in order to do this you must prepare to leave your comfort zone …"

FETCHING THE STICK
OF WISDOM

The night after that session with Dog, I couldn't sleep. The full moon beamed down into my bedroom, and I was restless. I lay awake, tossing and turning. I kept hearing dogs barking and howling from the surrounding hills. Or were they wolves? My mind was filled with untold nameless fears. I was truly experiencing the dark night of the soul; it seemed as if that night would never end. I didn't sleep a wink. By the morning, I was exhausted.

"Dog", I asked, as soon as the first light of dawn at last streaked the sky, "why does time seem to drag by so slowly when things are bad, like some form of torture, and yet it vanishes in an instant whenever I'm enjoying myself?"

DOG: "Ah yes, time. Well, basically you've got that all wrong too. According to your view of life, there is a past, a present and a future. But this is fundamentally wrong. There is only present; past and future are figments of your imagination. The essence of existence inhabits only the present moment, and that is precisely what you humans must do too.

"But instead, you rake over the past, and wallow in bitter regrets. You anticipate the future, and fill yourself with fear. If what is happening in this moment is good you want it to go on for ever, and you fear that it will not. If what is happening now is bad, you fear that it will continue in this way, and probably get worse. If things do get worse, you tell yourself that you knew this would happen; this is an aspect of your gift for self-fulfilling prophecy. If things improve, you forget about that next time.

"My teaching to you is to dwell fully in the present moment. Take each instant of life in your jaws, and chew it with all your strength; squeeze from it every drop of possibility, and then drop it immediately to seize the next moment. Be spontaneous. Be enthusiastic.

Live with abandon. Let go of all your petty little worries about life and death and paying your mortgage. Take risks. Live dangerously. Enjoy freedom. Life is neither too short nor too long. Life is exactly the right length.

🐾 "Pay attention to the example of my emissaries. Do the crazy things you always wanted to do, but were too timid, or too conventional, or just not crazy enough. Run naked into the sea in the middle of winter. Sniff someone's bottom to see what they've been up to. Run backward and forward in pointless zig-zig patterns. Get completely out of breath for no reason whatsoever. Bite people randomly and run away, laughing.

🐾 "This so-called 'civilisation' of yours is just far too complex. You've got to learn simplicity. And for goodness sake stop being so analytical. My emissaries have been playing games with you in this regard for many thousands of years. When you go away and leave them at home, they show that they always know when you are returning. You think this is really terrific, and it makes you feel very good. But they are not doing it to make you feel better. They are encouraging you to awaken your own ancient capacity for instinct and intuition.

🐾 "You must stop trying to achieve everything by thinking things through with your intellect, and start to use the really important faculties. You must develop your intuition, trust your instincts, follow your nose. Stop thinking about stuff all the time."

LIFE IN THE DOGHOUSE

DOG: "You think too much, and do too little. True spirituality lies in living life, not in pondering on the inner meaning of things. Loosen up! Are you getting the message?"

ME: "Let me think about that."

DOG: "Oh, and by the way … You give us silly names, like Spot or Rufus or Fido. We accept these names, just to humour you. But did you know that we also give you personalised names?"

ME: "No, actually, I didn't."

DOG: "Of course not. And this is because you have not bothered to learn our language, as we have done our best to learn yours."

ME (*intrigued*): "So what kind of names do you give us?"

DOG: "Purely descriptive names, such as 'Sits-on-his-bottom-all-day', or 'Doesn't-like-walking'. And your name roughly translates as 'Ashamed-of-genitals'. Did you know that?"

ME: "No, actually, I didn't.
Shall we take a break now?"

CLOSE TO THE BONE

I pondered on what Dog had said about freedom and spontaneity and being in the moment. And I tried it out. I did things on the spur of the moment. I deliberately made plans just so that I could abandon them later on and thus be spontaneously in the moment – it was relatively straightforward to come up with all kinds of

things I didn't want to do because I knew that I was going to drop them. I even sniffed a couple of people's bottoms when they weren't looking. But something was wrong. It still didn't feel quite right. It was time to talk to Dog again.

ME: "I'm having trouble with this spontaneity stuff. I'm doing new and exciting things, but something feels wrong.

I'm worried about what people are thinking. They look at me as if I'm mad. What can I do?"

DOG: "You are making progress. But I can see what your problem is. You see, you humans are constantly trying to create a certain impression about yourselves, rather than being as you really are. In the realm of Dog, what you see is what you get. Your computer people call this WYSIWYG. To speak in their language, dogs are like the Macintosh computers in life, while humans are the PCs. Your 'operating system' is strained, full of contradictions, and likely to crash at any moment, requiring complete reinstallation of spiritual software. Let me quote you some inspiration from the *Book of Dog*:

For lo, I say unto you: stay loose, man; let it all hang out.

POMERANIANS: CHAPTER 6, VERSE 1

PUPPY LOVE

 "The *Book of Dog* is exhorting you to get away from all your self-repression and heavy guilt trips. It's all to do with your sexuality; you're so ashamed of it. You're prudish, puritanical and totally in denial. You seem to forget that you're an animal like the rest of us. Sex is one of the great joys of life; furthermore, it's clearly needed for your survival as a species. Yet you're extremely ambivalent about it – you hide it away in dark secret places. You pretend that your parents don't do it. You don't do it enough, so it's on your mind all the time. You've even lost the ability to take care of the hygienic requirements of your own genitalia in the way that nature intended. Quite frankly, it's disgusting.

🐾 "The answer is very simple, really – you just have to be much more upfront about the whole thing. If you fancy someone, let them know about it. Get out there and do sex, then forget about it and get on with something else until you get another chance to do it again. Do it in the great outdoors, and forget about that dreadful missionary position thing. It isn't becoming, and you can't enjoy the view. Remember you're an animal, and for goodness sake start behaving like one.

🐾 "When you've dealt with this basic sex stuff, you'll find that there's a whole lot of other connected issues that will then get sorted out. For instance, you humans are so indirect about everything. You have all these convoluted procedures and protocols for everything. You're too damn complex. You don't say what you mean, and you don't mean what you say. And you all take yourselves far too seriously. You're so scared of seeming ridiculous. But you've got this whole thing the wrong way round, as usual. Being foolish

is good. Even some of your own great spiritual teachers have realised this, down through the ages. Being afraid of being ridiculous – that really is ridiculous. We all know this, but you don't. Was it not your own great writer Samuel Butler who said, 'The great pleasure of a dog is that you may make a fool of yourself with him; and not only will he not scold you, but he will make a fool of himself too'?

🐾 "When you have a problem, you buy a book on the subject, instead of doing something about it. Books like

This Book will Change your Life or *Enlightenment in Ten Minutes* or *Feel the Fear and Change your Underpants*. Most of the time you don't even read the book. How is that supposed to help?"

So I went out to try out my new-found instincts. It was great. I went to the park and saw this incredibly beautiful blonde. She was way out of my league, but I had a good feeling and I went for it, and the rest is history.

KEEPING THE WOLF
FROM THE DOOR

One day I woke up and thought, why don't I ask Dog about money and all that material stuff? So I did.

ME: "What about money and all that material stuff?"

DOG: "What about it?"

ME: "Well, why is money so problematic? Why do I never have enough of it? How can I get more?"

DOG: "I'm afraid you've got things wrong as usual. Money isn't important."

ME: "What is important, then?"

DOG: "There are only three things in life that are important, and only one of them is really, really important. The *Book of Dog* is very clear on this point. Let me direct you to the following words:

Now abideth Food, Exercise and Affection. But the greatest of these is Food. Though I am well loved and amply exercised, but have not food, I am as a sounding bell or a tinkling cymbal. And though I have the gift of toys, and understand all mysteries of how to outwit cats, and all knowledge of where bones are buried, and though I can move mountains of sticks from one spot to another, but have not Food, it profiteth me nothing. Food never faileth; but where there are dog-chews, they shall lose their taste. And where there are dog-toys, they shall fall apart. For now we see through a dog-flap darkly, but then face to face. When I was a pup, I understood as a pup; I thought as a pup. But when I became a dog, I put away puppyish things.

ST BERNARD'S EPISTLE TO THE ROTTWEILERS

"Now it's time for you humans to put away puppyish things. Put away your concern with fame and fortune and being sensible. It's time for you to grow up.

Getting enough to eat – that's where enlightenment is at. That's the single most important thing in life. Whatever it is, grab it and eat it, before anyone else does – that's the golden rule. That's the secret of success and happiness."

ME: "But what is the point of life? Why are we here? What is our higher purpose? What great cosmic goal are we here to achieve?"

DOG: "The purpose of life is not to do anything. It isn't to achieve anything, or to understand anything. The purpose is to be. That's your goal in life – to just Be. That's what my emissaries have been trying to teach you for hundreds of thousands of years.

"And another thing. Stop being such fussy eaters. Don't push your food around on the plate. Just eat it. Don't worry about chewing. Gulp it down. Then look for something else to eat. Do I make myself clear?"

ME: "I'm feeling hungry. Can we stop now?"

DOG: "Good. By the way, did you know that dogs are very powerful magicians?"

ME: "No, I didn't."

DOG: "Oh yes. They're particularly skilled at making things disappear. Usually by eating them."

STRAINING AT LIFE'S LEASH

D og's guidance was not turning out quite as I had expected. Furthermore, I wasn't getting a chance to ask very many questions. This pattern continued with the next session.

DOG: "And here's another thing that's wrong with you. You're nervous, angst-ridden and torn apart by doubt, and you have this weird habit of nervously biting your nails. For goodness sake, bite something more substantial, preferably belonging to someone else.

"And you must constantly strive to reach ever higher goals, and never give up no matter how unattainable they may seem. We call this process developing 'the Higher Shelf'. No matter how out of reach it may be, no matter how impossible it may seem to get at what is up there, you must keep on striving for it. That is the spirit of Dog. Don't be so cautious and careful, paranoid and wretchedly systematic about everything, and lazy and worried about getting too tired out.

🐾 "Be exuberant. Be spontaneous. Be erratic. Do random, free-form things. Expend energy on senseless nonsense. This is the way to live life. These are the things to strive for in life: the tenacity of the terrier, the spiritedness of the spaniel, the simplicity of the schnauzer, the chutzpah of the chihuahua. These are the truly timeless qualities to which you must aspire."

🐾 "You're so scared of everything, from walking through stinging nettles to dipping your toe into cold water. You really need to work on this. So here's your homework. By our next session, I want you to go out and pick a fight with a massive and hugely superior opponent. Will you do that for me?"

ME: "Let me get back to you on that one."

BONES OF CONTENTION

In the following session, Dog still seemed to have a lot on his mind.

DOG: "Next problem. You humans want to change things just for the sake of change. True wisdom, as demonstrated by my emissaries, is to get things the way you want them, be happy with that, and fight to the death to keep them that way. We call it 'creative conservatism'.

"Where territory is concerned, you humans are pathetic. When it comes to defending anything, you delegate all your responsibility to governments and criminals and armies.

"You're all so frightened of conflict. Yet conflict is essential in order to establish the order of things. That's its purpose: true fighting is a profoundly spiritual pursuit, as recognised by your samurai. The universe is a fundamentally ordered phenomenon. At least, it was before you people came along, leaving chaos and endless restructuring in your wake. In reality there is a rightful place for everything and everyone.

🐾 "That's why we need a recognisable hierarchy of authority. We need to know who's in charge. We have to be aware of the pecking order – which people we can put pressure on and mercilessly subdue, and which people can do that to us. We need to honour mastery and obedience. If we don't have such a system in place, we will waste our lives in interminable petty squabbles and continual reassessment of the whole basis of society."

ME: "Mmmm…"

MAN'S BEST FRIEND

Following session: Dog asked me a question! But still I had no chance to get a word in edgeways …

DOG: "I have something particularly important to talk to you about today. Why do you think it is that my emissaries are universally known as 'man's best friend'?

ME: "Well …"

DOG: "Simply because we are better friends to you than other humans are. We behave like this to set you an example. We are trustworthy, dependable and loyal unto death. We are endlessly charitable, appreciative and forgiving. As your enlightened Sufi mystic Sa'di remarked in 1298 AD (Anno Doggo 13694): 'A dog will never forget the crumb thou gavest him, though thou may'st afterwards throw a hundred stones at his head.' Whatever horrors you perpetrate upon us, we still follow you, trust you, assist you, defend you, like you and continue to be your friend. We are paragons of honesty, genuineness and simple straightforwardness. Hypocrisy and double standards have no place in our vocabulary. We are unconditional love incarnate.

"You know in your heart that when you neglect us, we give you more affection. When you say a harsh word to us, we lick your face. When you kick us round the room, we love you with even greater devotion. And yet you do not learn from this."

What could I say? I was astonished, and profoundly moved by these words of passion and sincerity. And I knew, once and for all, from the bottom of my being, that Dog is Love.

DOG: "And by the way, it's time you people started mutual face-licking. It would do your international relations a power of good."

LET SLEEPING DOGS LIE

Eventually, I plucked up courage and determined to ask Dog one question – the big one. So the following morning, after a nourishing breakfast of lamb chops, leg of pork and sirloin steak, I said: "Dog, I desperately need to know this. Why do I have so much trouble with intimate relationships? Why do so many other people have trouble with relation-ships? Will I ever find my dream partner, and live happily ever after?" This was his reply:

DOG: "You think that you have relationships so that you can feel loved, obtain a regular supply of sex, and not be alone. This is not so. The real reason that you have relationships is to discover your shortcomings – to have your buttons pushed, find out about your unresolved issues, and have things about yourself brought into the open that you have been spending your life hiding from other people. Only then can you deal with them, and grow. Even then, you humans will still be hopeless at being in relationships, for you seem very slow to learn. So you need guidance. You need a role model for how to be in a relationship. And that is where my Earthly representatives come in.

🐾 "My emissaries have very simple needs and wants: they want their food; they want to go out and run about a lot; and they want to have company, preferably that of their owner, whom they love quite unconditionally. As long as they get these things (plus maybe sex in the open air once in a while) they are completely happy. They don't suddenly say to themselves, 'This isn't what I wanted after all; what I want now is something completely different'. They don't keep

moving the goalposts all the time. Dogs are the perfect models for being in a relationship; the reason why I originally manifested myself through them on your planet was to aid you in this way. I decided that the best way to do this would be to let your ancestors think that you were 'domesticating' us. Unfortunately, very few humans ever realised that this is why dogs spend time with them, and even fewer have managed to apply the lessons.

🐾 "Cats, in contrast to us, are independent, contrary, changeable, demanding and unpredictable. Way back in time, cats realised that dogs had pretty much sewn up the straightforward/dependable/know-where-you-are-with-them relationship stuff, so they decided to do something completely different. They reckoned that they would portray to humans how not to be in a relationship. If cats aren't made a fuss of every hour or so, they will quite readily call the whole relationship off – at least until the next time they're hungry. To emphasise the point, they'll only eat the most expensive cat-food. If they want to make a major issue of it, they'll go off their food altogether, and possibly die. That's it in a nutshell.

"Sad to say, most of humanity gets this whole thing completely the wrong way round, and emulates cats rather than dogs in their relationships. But then that's one of the dangers when you are the dominant species on the planet, and have free will into the bargain. And the tragedy is that many of you do worse still, and use other creatures as your inspirational role models – notably the ostrich, the stick insect and the snapping turtle."

BACK TO BASICS

I was undoubtedly learning a great deal from these messages. But now I yearned for some even more profound information. I wanted an overview of the whole future of humankind. So I asked Dog for his thoughts on this. This was his reply:

DOG: "Let me answer you with another inspirational passage from the *Book of Dog*:

In the beginning, Dog created heaven and earth. And the earth was without form, and void. And Dog said, Let there be smell; and everything was very smelly. And Dog smelt everything that he had made, and it was very good.

POODLENESIS: CHAPTER 1, VERSE 1

"What these words are saying to you is this. The real problem with humanity is that you think you're an incredibly evolved species, but in fact your evolution is going backwards. You used to have a keen sense of smell, sharp eyesight and excellent hearing. You could survive in the wild. You had four decent legs, and could run fast. And you had a proper tail, like everybody else. Now look at you! You've degenerated. All these bits and pieces have atrophied away to nothing.

 "If you're going to get anywhere, you've got to reverse this process. And this is the reason why you've now developed techniques for genetic modification: it's so that you can regain these features and faculties, without taking millions of years to do so. You can once more become practically designed creatures. You can develop ears that will stick up on top of your head and rotate in different directions. You can get a strong jaw and some serious teeth. You can drive along in your car with your nose sticking out the window, smelling stories on the wind. And you can once more have a tail. Why? So that you can wag it, of course."

LET'S NOT BE DOGMATIC

As the sessions continued, I had begun to notice that Dog had an uncanny ability to know what was on my mind, even without me having to ask. It was extraordinary. But what was absolutely amazing was that I also began to know what Dog was going to say to me! Perhaps I was at last beginning to develop my own intuitive and instinctive faculties, just as Dog had told me I should. So eventually Dog would say something like:

"You're completely hopeless at licking your plate after you've finished eating. This may seem like a relatively trivial matter, but from the point of cosmic responsibility it is of the profoundest spiritual importance."

And I would say something like: " I knew you were going to say that."

And Dog would say: "I knew you knew that I was going to say that. I decided to say it anyway."

And I would say: "This is getting us nowhere."

But then Dog said: "On the contrary, it is getting us somewhere. I have been waiting so long for you to reach this point. Now you are finally beginning to understand. This is crucially important, don't you see? For when you have a question to ask me, and you know what the answer will be, then you won't need me to answer it for you."

My mind raced. "But that means …" I began.

"Yes." Dog replied. "It means that you can answer the question yourself."

"And that means …" I interjected.

"Exactly", said Dog, reading my mind once more, "it means that you don't have to ask the question."

"Wow!" I cried. "And …"

"… you don't need to have any real conversations with me. You can just write down the answers yourself. You can put down anything you want."

ME (*shocked*): "You mean, make it up?"

DOG: "Yes."

ME (*thinking fast*): "Are you implying that you …"

DOG: " …make this stuff up too? What difference would it make? Anything that's been created, somewhere back along the line, somebody has to have made up. So why not me?"

ME: "But that's awful. How can I believe any of what you've been telling me if you've just been making it all up?"

DOG: "Well, if nobody made anything up, there wouldn't be anything, would there?"

ME: "I suppose you're right."

DOG: "You're damn right I'm right. So you can make this stuff up, too."

ME: "I can?"

DOG: "You can. And you can publish it."

ME: "And people will read it?"

DOG: "People will read it."

ME: "People will buy it?"

DOG: "They will buy it. Trust me. People want this stuff desperately."

ME: "But will I be able to…"

DOG: "Don't worry. Just make it up."

ME: "And what about …"

DOG: "It won't be a problem."

ME: "And …"

DOG: "That will be okay too."

🐾 This was incredible.

ME: "Just one other thing …"

DOG: "What?"

ME: "Does that mean I'm becoming psychic?"

DOG: "No."

That was a real surprise, I have to say.

THE END OF THE TAIL

After that, it seemed irrelevant to ask any more questions. I had learned an extraordinary amount. It seemed as if we had covered everything in the world that there was to know about. And I had taken it all on board. My life had changed so much. I was happier, fitter, leaner and stronger. I was enthusiastic and bursting with vitality.

🐾 Every single day I'd wake up bright and refreshed, jump out of bed, leap for joy, run round the block a couple of dozen times, evacuate my bowels with ease, and wolf down an enormous high-protein breakfast that never

included less than four types of raw meat, which my butcher had now got used to supplying on the bone. I had a wonderful gang of male friends with whom I'd regularly go out and cruise round the neighbourhood looking for trouble, occasionally roughing up people who really asked for it. We'd put these characters in their place, and they'd rarely step out of line again. It was strictly for the good of the local community, of course. I had no shortage of girlfriends, and my difficulty with long-term involvement no longer bothered me. My ex-wife's interest miraculously revived when she encountered my new-found *joie-de-vivre* and vigour. At regular intervals, she'd invite me round for intimate encounters; I'd be happy to call by for a bit of action, but made it quite clear that I wasn't interested in serious commitment. There were just too many other juicy bones to pick, elsewhere.

FANGS FOR THE MEMORY

And so in what was to be my final session with Dog, I determined to voice my gratitude.

ME: "I want to thank you, Dog, for all that you have given me. I feel deep gratitude welling up from the bottom of my heart for all this inspiration and guidance. How can I begin to express my appreciation?"

DOG: "Yes, I have given you much. And you have learned well. So here is how you can thank me. I want you to take this information from our conversations, and make of it a book. A book that will change people's lives, a book that will be read by millions; a book that will feature in the bestseller lists. I want you to call this book *Conversations with Dog* …"

ME: "That's a good title …"

DOG: "… Shut up and listen. This book represents your destiny – your pet project, as it were. You have been personally selected (though I've no idea why) as the vehicle for this great spiritual venture.

"I know it sounds far-fetched – implawsible even – but this great book will only be the beginning, for there is so much more to be revealed

to humankind through you. So there will be more volumes of my wisdom after this, books that you have not dreamed of. There will be *More Conversations with Dog* and *Even More Interesting Conversations with Dog*. There will be *Intimate Conversations with Dog* and *Incredibly Amazing Conversations with Dog* and *Conversations with Dog in the Kitchen*. There will be *Discourses with Dog*, *Discussions with Dog* and *Dialogues with Dog*. Yes, I particularly like those ones; they have a nice ring to them. There will be Dog Diaries, Dog Workbooks and Dog Encyclopaedias. There will be workshops, seminars, author tours, study groups; CD-ROMs, videos, tee-shirts and different kinds of spiritual merchandise. We will not rest until every automobile in the land has in its rear window a beautiful cuddly nodding Conversing Dog™. I can see it now. This thing is going to be very big. It will become your life's work. You're going to be very busy. But then, in your newly enlightened canine way, how could you want it any other way? And besides, you'll probably also become influential, famous, rich and well-loved by millions of people the world over."

ME: "Hey, I can live with that."

THE TEN COMMANDMENTS

1 Do anything you can get away with.
2 If you're guilty, look guilty. But do it again when nobody's looking.
3 Never trust a stranger.
4 Eat disgusting things without ever getting sick.
5 Always gobble your neighbour's breakfast, your neighbour's lunch, your neighbour's dinner, titbits, snacklets and treats.
6 Adopt the most comfortable chair as your own indisputable territory.
7 Have sex in public places.
8 Go forth and multiply.
9 Protect your space at all costs.
10 Never give up.

Other books by Gerry Maguire Thompson:

Cats are from Venus, Dogs are from Mars
The Mind/Body/Spirit Internet Guide
The Atlas of the New Age
Feng Shui for Dogs
The Celtic Oracle Set
The Weekend Shaman & Other New Age Types
Meditation Made Easy
Astral Sex to Zen Teabags
Feng Shui Astrology for Lovers
The Encyclopedia of the New Age
The Shiatsu Manual

Gerry Maguire Thompson can be contacted at:
11 Jew Street, Brighton, East Sussex, BN1 IUT

gerry@pavilion.co.uk
www.zenteabags.com

ACKNOWLEDGEMENTS

I am profoundly indebted to Debbie Thorpe for
commissioning this rare treasure of a book.

I am eternally grateful to Jane Alexander for nurturing the project
throughout its course from fragile inception to fruitful completion.

How can I ever thank Katey Day enough for the miracle
of her editorial input to this magnum opus?

My gratitude to Claire Warde for adroitly guiding the work
out to its loving readers, through the vital stages of publicity
and promotion, extends to the stars and beyond.

There is no way that I can sufficiently thank the noble and heroic
folks at Bridgewater Books for their infinite resources in designing
and laying out the book in all its pristine, shining brilliance.

The support and succour of Elaine Grace Bellamy is a constant
and inspirational wonder for which I cannot begin to offer
high enough praise in this or any other lifetime.

I am pathetically incapable of ever coming near to expressing
the tiniest fraction of the appropriate appreciation to
Maddie Hardie for the bijou and exultantly colourful
illustrations that adorn every page of this glorious masterpiece.

I honour and treasure you, my adoring readers, for your
inestimable generosity, shrewd judgement and sound
investment sense in purchasing this book.

And I am deeply in love with myself.